THOR, WITH ANGELS

CHRISTOPHER FRY

THOR, WITH ANGELS
A Play

Geoffrey Cumberlege
OXFORD UNIVERSITY PRESS
LONDON   NEW YORK   TORONTO

Oxford University Press, Amen House, London E.C.4

GLASGOW NEW YORK TORONTO MELBOURNE WELLINGTON
BOMBAY CALCUTTA MADRAS CAPE TOWN

Geoffrey Cumberlege, Publisher to the University

*First performed at the Canterbury Festival
in June 1948.
In an Acting Edition published by H. J.
Goulden Ltd. for the Friends of Canterbury
Cathedral the text of the play was first issued
in 1948.*

*Second Impression (Oxford University Press) 1949
Third Impression (reset) 1949
Fourth Impression 1950*

To

E. MARTIN BROWNE

and the Tewkesbury summer 1939

CHARACTERS

CYMEN

CLODESUIDA, *His Wife*

MARTINA, *His Daughter*

QUICHELM, *His Elder Son*

CHELDRIC, *His Younger Son*

TADFRID ⎫
OSMER ⎬ *His Brothers-in-Law*

COLGRIN, *His Steward*

ANNA, *Colgrin's Wife*

HOEL, *A British Prisoner*

MERLIN

A MESSENGER

SCENE: *A Jutish Farmstead,* A.D. 596

A Jutish farmstead, both within and without. To the left a group of trees; to the right a shed, in which COLGRIN, *an elderly man, is asleep among the straw. Enter* QUICHELM. *He hammers at the farm door.*

QUICHELM. Hyo, there! Who's awake? Where's
    The welcome of women for warfarers?
    Where's my Wodenfearing mother?
    Hey! hey! Spare some sleep for us:
    Leave us half a snore and a stale dream.
    Here's your battery of males come home!
    Our bones are aching; we're as wet
    As bogworms. Who's alive in there?

COLGRIN. There's an infernal clatter. What's the matter?
    Foof! Straw in the nostrils. That's bad.
    Who's blaspheming in the thick of the mist?
    I've got you on my weapon's point.
    (Where the Valhalla is it?)

QUICHELM.   Colgrin,
    You scrawny old scurfscratcher, is that you?

COLGRIN. Frog-man, fen-fiend, werewolf, oul, elf,
    Or whatever unnatural thing you are
    Croaking in the voice of Master Quichelm
    Who I happen to know is away waging war,
    Stand away from the swiping of my sword.
    (Where in thunder did I put it?)

QUICHELM. Runt of an old sow's litter, you slop-headed
    Pot-scourer, come here, you buckle-backed
    Gutsack, come out of there!

COLGRIN.   That's
    The young master. There's not a devil
    In the length of the land could pick such a posy of words

And not swoon smelling it. Here I come,
Here I come. Welcome home and so forth.

QUICHELM. Woden welt you for a sheeptick, where's my mother?

COLGRIN. That's a nice question. I must ponder.
Maybe asleep in her cot. Or not.

QUICHELM. I'll carve your dropsical trunk into a tassel.
Where's my sister? You were left to guard them,
Not to roll your pig-sweat in a snoring stupor.
Tell me where they are before I unbutton your throat.

MARTINA [*entering*]. We're here, Quichelm. I knew you'd come
to-day.
The cows this morning were all facing north.
Are you whole and hale?

QUICHELM.   Look me over. Ten
Fingers. You can take the toes for granted.
Where's my mother?

MARTINA.   We went to early rite.
I wanted to stay and keep a watch out for you
But she made me go; you know what she is.

COLGRIN. That's what I said. Gone to early rite.
And my wife with her; a devout woman, but dismal
In some respects. They'll be back just now.
The sun's arisen.

QUICHELM.   You get stuck
Into some work, you whitebellied weasel.
By dugs, I think I'll strike you anyway.

COLGRIN. Wasn't I there as bright and bristling
As Barney the boarhound, just as soon as I heard
Your honour's foot creak over the bridge?

[2]

MARTINA. Beat him to-morrow. Let's be affable.
Is father all right? And Cheldric?

QUICHELM.   Cheldric's all right.

MARTINA. Why not father? Stop picking at your teeth.
Something is wrong. Was father killed?
I knew it. The house was crowned with crows this morning.

QUICHELM. Shut up. None of us is killed.
Are you still here?

COLGRIN [*going in*]. No, sir, no. It's what
You remember of me. There's trouble coming. I see that.

Enter CLODESUIDA *and* ANNA.

CLODESUIDA. Quichelm, you're back! Oh, fortunate day.

ANNA. Welcome home.

QUICHELM.   Yes, the battle's finished.

CLODESUIDA [*to* ANNA]. Rouse the fire up; and find them food.
                              [*Exit* ANNA.

MARTINA. Don't expect pleasure.

CLODESUIDA.   Something is wrong. Is your father
With you, and well?

QUICHELM.   He's much as when you saw him.

CLODESUIDA. Much? What's that, much? Has he been hurt?

QUICHELM. No weapon has touched him.

CLODESUIDA.   Then he's ill?
Why do you talk to me in a kind of cloud?
What has happened?

QUICHELM.   Mother, we breathe cloud.
It's the chief product of this island.

[3]

CLODESUIDA.   Don't provoke me!
Where is your father?

QUICHELM.   Coming up the hill.

MARTINA. Dimly, yes; I can just see the shapes of them.

CLODESUIDA. And Cheldric, too? And your uncles?
Yes,
They all come. The mist is confusing. I could imagine
There are five of them.

QUICHELM.   So there are. My father
Brings a prisoner.

CLODESUIDA.   A prisoner? Are we
To have an intolerable Saxon here?

QUICHELM. An even greater strain on your toleration:
A Briton. A British slave who fought for the Saxons.

CLODESUIDA. But why? Why bring a benighted Briton here?
I thought those heathen had been tidied away, once
And for all. And the country's healthier for it.
Your father's demented.

QUICHELM.   You would have said so
If you had seen him as we saw him in the battle.
Like a madman, he saved this Briton when we'd have killed him:
Burst in among us, blaspheming against Woden,
Broke his sword in the air—he swore it broke
Against a staggering light—and stood roaring,
Swaying in a sweat of wax, bestraddled
Over the fallen Briton. And then, as though
The beast which had bragged in his brain had leapt away,
Became himself again,
Only in a fury with the light which broke his sword.

CLODESUIDA. How could the sword have broken?

[4]

You make me afraid
To see him. Are you sure that he blasphemed?
That's the worst of all. It's hard enough
To live well-thought-of by the gods.

MARTINA. We haven't
Enough cattle to placate them more than twice a year.
He knows we have to be careful.

QUICHELM. They're here. And you haven't heard the worst.

CLODESUIDA. The worst? What worse can there be?
Quichelm,
What else? . . .

QUICHELM. Don't let him know that I've been talking.
He'd lay me flat.

CLODESUIDA. He'll notice how I tremble.

[*Enter to the house* CYMEN, *his brothers-in-law* TADFRID
and OSMER, *and his younger son* CHELDRIC. CLODE-
SUIDA *and* MARTINA *stand staring at him.*

CYMEN. Well? Have I come home? Or is this a place
Of graven images? What's the silence for?
I've laid down arms, so that arms
Could take me up, a natural expectation.
Where's my wife?

CLODESUIDA. You can see me. Here I am.

CYMEN. Where's my wife? Where's the head on my breast?
Better. Where's my daughter? Where's the white
Hand hanging on my shoulder? Better, better.
I'll have a cup of mead.
Where's my mead? Where the devil's my mead?
Have I got to wring the water out of my shirt
To get a drink?

[5]

COLGRIN [*appearing*]. Here's your mead, my lord:
And the bees were proud to make themselves drunk
To make you drunk, and welcome home, my lord,
And Woden worship you and your victory,
Hear, hear!

CYMEN.   Loki lacerate you for a liar
And my foot in your teeth.

COLGRIN.   Quite so, exactly.

CYMEN. Wash my feet. Well, here's gut-comfort, anyway.
Who can be called defeated who can still imbibe
And belch?

CLODESUIDA. Defeated? Have you come back defeated
When I sacrificed a good half-goat. . . .

CYMEN.   No doubt
The wrong half, my jewel: the hind-quarters,
And it brought us rumping home. Well,
I'm still good enough for a bad joke.
Liquor. Down the throat, sunshine; hum
A lazy day to my inside. I'll doze
In the meadow of my stomach. There's no warmth in a wife.

CLODESUIDA. Who turns me cold? What besides defeat
Have you still to tell me?

CYMEN.   Ask the dumb icebergs behind you.
Take stock of those long jowls, my jewel,
Those ruminating thundercoloured bulls
Your brothers: and our pastry-pallid sons
Who look on their father with such filial
Disapproval. A fine resentful march
This night has been, with no moon and no
Conversation: nothing to break the monotony
Except Tadfrid spitting once in every mile

[6]

And twenty-seven gurks from Osmer.
Spit some words at me instead, and gurk
Away your grudge. I'm tired of this subterranean
Muttering. Where's that water? My feet want comfort.

TADFRID. That's what this house will want before long, and may
Our guilt be forgiven us.

CLODESUIDA.   What kind of talk is this?

CYMEN. Tell her, tell her. I'm humble.

CLODESUIDA.   Do you say that?
Guilt, forgiveness, humility? What next?
Are you mad?

CYMEN.   Tell her I am or you'll strangle yourselves
With an unspoken truth.

CLODESUIDA.   Has none of you the courage
To speak?

TADFRID. Even though he's our overlord,
And though he may not at the time have been fully responsible—

OSMER. Let me tell her, Tadfrid; I speak faster.
It was approaching dusk, last evening.
We were catching a bright victory in our caps,
When Eccha, the earl, was killed by a thrust from the spear
Of this British brat:
And we were at the boy in the bat of an eye
To give him joy of our vengeance and a shove
To doom and a damned journey into dust,
When Cymen, our chief, our lord, your maleficent
Male—

CLODESUIDA. Though you're my brother I'll beat your mouth
If it passes a lie!

TADFRID.   It's the truth that he says.

[7]

OSMER.   All right.
It's the truth that I say. Like a bear-sark blundering
He hit up our downcoming swords, sprang in
As white as a water-spout spinning in a full moon,
Shouting 'The gods can go and beg for blood!
Let 'em learn of us!'

TADFRID.   Word for word. 'Let 'em learn
Of us.'

CLODESUIDA. It's certain they heard!

OSMER.   From that moment, you
    could feel it,
The sky turned round, Ceaulin's men broke through,
Thor, in the scarlet dusk, swore and swung,
And Woden rode in rancour, as well he might,
And trod upon our dead.

TADFRID.   And so we slogged
Out from defeat, and he lugged the Briton with him.

CLODESUIDA. Is it believable?

CHELDRIC.   Look, father's weeping.

QUICHELM. A nice inheritance we have, all watermarked
With tears.

CLODESUIDA. Who's this man, spilling sawdust
Like an old puppet? I never saw him till now.
You make me ashamed, in front of our sons.

CYMEN.   Can't I
Have tears of rage? Why not the hot spout
Of indignation? Is it better to spew?
By the thousand and three thews of the muscular god,
Some fiend of this land came at my back!
I was thrown by a trick.

[8]

TADFRID.   He should stand in the winter sea
    Till his clothes freeze to his flesh. It's the only way
    To be sure of a store of magic against such an evil.

CLODESUIDA. And catch death? That's an efficacious magic
    If you like. It's more decently religious
    To offer a sacrifice, than to offer himself
    To an early grave.

OSMER.   What devil was it that damned him
    To its own design? Can he tell us that?

CYMEN.   Some ancient
    Damp god of this dooming island, who spat
    The fungus out of his mouth and caught me napping.
    I curse this kingdom, water, rock and soil!
    I accuse and curse the creaking of its boughs
    And the slaver on the mouth of its winds! It makes
    A fool of me! Too many voices rasp
    Out of decaying rafters, out of every cave
    And every hole in the yellow sodden hills.
    This is the golden future our fathers died for!
    The gods look at it! Here's the slice of fortune
    They came to carve with their courage
    When they pitched themselves on the narrow, shuddering sea
    To deal and duck death under the hanging chalk.
    I stack my curses on those first rich rumours
    Which fetched us here, rollicking with ambition.
    I curse the muck and gravel where we walk.
    I'd curse each singular soaking blade of grass
    Except that a grey hair ties me for time.
    Here we live, in our fathers' mirage.
    Cities, they'd heard of, great with columns,
    Gay cities, where wealth was bulging the doors
    And the floors were sagging with the weight of gold.

[9]

The orchards rang with fruit, the hills moved
With grain like a lion's mane, and wherever
A river sauntered the fish swam, and eels
Reeled in bright mud. Flocks were fair,
And cows like pendulous fountains of alabaster
Went lowing over land where silver skulked
Waiting for skill; a land where summer days
Could call to one another across the night
Under the northern pole. So here we live
And choke in our father's mirage. Dreams they were,
As well we know; we live in the skull
Of the beautiful head which swam in the eyes of our fathers.
Our ploughshares jag on the stumps of moonwhite villas.
And my brain swerves with the sudden sting of one
Of the island gods, the down-and-out divinities
Moping, mildewed with immortality,
Cross-boned on weedy altars. I curse this land
That curses me!

OSMER.   Then cut yourself clear of its curse
And win this house again for Woden, before
We all know worse.

                    [*He drags forward* HOEL, *the Briton.*
                    Here's the land you loathe,
In bone and blood. Break its back.

CLODESUIDA.   We have always
Been god-fearing, but now it appears he fears
More gods than he knows what to do with. What can we do?

TADFRID. Obliterate the cause of sin. Do the undeed,
The death-lack which lost us our victory.
Where's the difficulty?

OSMER.   There is no difficulty.
Here's the quivering black-haired flesh,

[10]

As live as it was that time our blades were on him.
Well, we swing back on time, and hope the gods
Forget the indecision.

TADFRID.   It may seem now
To be somewhat in cold blood, but in fact his death
Was given to him in the battle yesterday;
This is merely the formal ceremony, which was overlooked.

QUICHELM. Kill him; make us respectable again.
I feel that all the gods are looking at us.

CHELDRIC. Do, father, kill him, as any other fellow's
Father would.

CLODESUIDA. Not inside the house!
The walls would never let his death go out.

CYMEN. No, nor anywhere here, I'll tell you all
Darker things yet. I have a great fear.

CLODESUIDA. Fear? Will you say that to the ears of your sons?

CYMEN. I say I fear myself, or rather
That not-myself which took my will,
Which forced a third strange eye into my head
So that I saw the world's dimensions altered.
I know no defence against that burst of fire.
[*To* HOEL.] You can tell me; what flogged away my strength,
What furtive power in your possession
Pulled the passion of my sword? Name that devil!
I'll have our gods harry him through the gaps
Between the stars, to where not even fiends
Can feed. Name him!

HOEL.   Who? Who am I to name?
I swear to God I know nothing of what you mean.

CYMEN. What God is that? You swear to a God?
What God?

[11]

HOEL. It was my grandfather who knew him well.
The One God, he's called. But I can't remember
The details; it's a long time ago that I saw
My grandfather, and I'm the last life
Of my family.

OSMER.   Send him where the moles
Can teach him to dig in the dark.

TADFRID.   His brows are marked
With the night already; douse the rest of him
And let's get to bed.

CYMEN.   Why shouldn't we give you the mercy
You showed to Eccha our earl?

HOEL.   It was all in the way
Of battle. I only expelled him from the world
As I let out my breath singing to the fame
Of Britain.

TADFRID. The fame of Britain! The fame of Britain
Is sung by us now. Let him echo Eccha
Into death, with the same ease.

OSMER.   Easy death,
Easy as shutting a door!

CYMEN.   This door shan't shut
Till I find what devil keeps it.

OSMER.   Then, by plague,
I'll void my vows of allegiance to this damned house!

TADFRID. And I; like a rat I'll run
Before the water rises.

CLODESUIDA.   Do you forget
Your wife and children? A sacrifice, Cymen,
This one sacrifice for our peace of mind.

[12]

CYMEN. What peace can we have until I know
   Whether or not the same misshapen fire again
   Will burn me? I've still got rags of reason
   To make our stark apprehension decent,
   And you shall be modest with me, or else bad-luck
   Will leer at the lot of us. If we kill him and bury him,
   I shall fill my lungs with relief and forget my fault
   And the flame will be on me while I whistle at a clear sky.
   No! This walking wound in my strength can walk on,
   Wake me in the morning, see me to my bed;
   He shall stand between me and the door so that his shadow
   Falls across everything I do: so every
   Moment shall have spears addressed to that dark
   Which lies in wait for my will. Alive,
   He's ours; dead, who knows to what
   Unfriendly power he will have given himself?
   Scowl at your own stampede of panic,
   Not at me. Look; the sun puts down
   The mist at last and looks out across the day.
   Here comes the burning sea of honey
   Over the grey sand of our defeat.
   We'll salute the sun that makes us men.
   Fill up the cups! [*To* COLGRIN.]
   O gigantic heart, beating in the breast of the sky,
   Lordlust the white-hot lion of the air,
   We are the men of the earth; our metal shouts
   With light only for you. (For chick's sake,
   Fill 'em up, fill 'em up!)—
   Give us huge harvest, potency and dominion.
   Make us pluck all from the teeth of this island.
   My strength comes back. By splendour,
   I'll send fear sprawling. By the zenith, I'll set
   My foot on the neck of the dark and get the gods

[13]

Again. [*He throws* HOEL *to the ground and puts his foot on his neck.*]
        Glory of life, I live!
We'll drink to our restored prosperity:
The sustaining sinews of tremendous Thor:
The unwearying, turbulent, blazing loins of Woden!
We raise our cups and drink, to the power of the gods,
This toast:
               'Let us love one another.'
         [*His cup falls from his hand. He stands trembling.*

OSMER. What madness is this?

CLODESUIDA.   What words are these?

TADFRID.   He has fallen
  Foul of his brain again, protect us!

CHELDRIC.   'Let us
  What,' did father say?

QUICHELM.   'Love one another';
  What a way to honour the gods!

CLODESUIDA.   He's not himself.
  It's the patter of delirium he talks;
  A lack of sleep.

CYMEN.   I'm in good health!
  No-one shall excuse this fiend that twists my tongue,
  By saying I'm sick! Show, show, show,
  Devil! By the first yowl of the world's first babe
  I'll be the master of my own voice!
  Show! Come out of your secret place and let me
  See you climb to my sword. This time it means
  Death, your precious Briton's end, I kill him!
        [*He makes to kill* HOEL, *but his sword is against* QUIC-
        HELM.]

QUICHELM. Father!

[14]

CLODESUIDA.   No! Hold him! He's battle-blind.

OSMER. You madman, it's your son, Quichelm. What's
The matter? Here's the road you have to take,
The black-haired enemy. Turn here.

CYMEN.   It seems
All one, it seems all one. There's no distinction.
Which is my son?

QUICHELM.   Can't you see me?
I'm your son.

CYMEN.   And my enemy,
My own flesh. My sword knew you. Deny it:
My sword understood. Distinction has gone!

CLODESUIDA. Take him and make him sleep; it must be
The burning of his body. I'll not believe
He is mad. Get him to rest and sleep. Dip him
In sleep, that blue well where shadows walk
In water over their heads, and he'll be washed
Into reason. This has taken my strength, too.

CYMEN. All right, I'll sleep. I'll count myself as over
For a while. But let not you, not one of you,
Step between me and what's to come. This house
Is on my back; it goes my way. Dare nothing
Against the Briton, or dread will stay with you
Forever, like pock-marks. We'll master this mystery.
His death can keep; his death can wait for me.
          [*Exeunt* CLODESUIDA, CYMEN, QUICHELM, CHELDRIC.

OSMER. And we're kept jangling in the pocket of uncertainty
While Woden wonders how to spend us.

TADFRID.   And sleep
Will lay us open to all the supernatural riffraff

[15]

That ever came crawling out of cobwebs. Pleasant
Dreams.

OSMER [*to* COLGRIN]. Take him to the barn.
Hanging for you, if he escapes.

COLGRIN. A rope isn't my style. I haven't the neck for it.
[*Exeunt* OSMER *and* TADFRID.

COLGRIN. Lowest form of life; that's you. Next to lowest, me.
So you can show respect. We'll make the barn
A guard-room. Get inside. This dizzy-dazzy
World made of morning sun and fog-spittle
Is nothing to do with you. Orders are otherwise.

HOEL. Try to think of it: I might by now
Have been wading about in the sway of death,
But I'm blinking at the light; my head swims with it.

COLGRIN. It doesn't do a man any good, daylight.
It means up and doing, and that means up to no good.
The best life is led horizontal
And absolutely unconscious. Get inside!
You flick of muck off the back hoof of a mule!
There's a point in being sworn at; it gives you something
To hand on to your fellow men. Now mind,
No monkey-tricks, no trying to escape,
I've got you covered—if I knew where I'd put my weapon.

HOEL. Where do you think I should escape to?

COLGRIN.   Why,
You'd skit off home.

HOEL.   That's where I've just escaped from
When I escaped death. Here I lie—
Hanging on to what was once my country,
Like an idiot clinging to the body of his dead mother.
Why don't you hack me off her? Why don't you?

[16]

Fool I was, fool I was, not to hug their swords
When they bore down on me. Why don't I settle
To a steady job in the grave, instead of this damned
Ambition for life, which doesn't even offer
A living wage? I want to live, even
If it's like a louse on the back of a sheep, skewering
Into the wool away from the beaks of crows;
Even like a limpet on a sour rock.
I want to live!

COLGRIN.   Me too;
Horizontal and absolutely unconscious.
But they keep us at it, they keep us at it.

Enter ANNA.

ANNA. Who at it? Not you at it. Don't you
Think he's ever at it; nobody's at it
Except old Anna. The farm's a hive
Of indolence: the place might as well be rubble.
Six upstanding men lying down, and nine
Cows lowing themselves into a cream cheese.

[*She goes into the barn to take down the washing from where
it hangs on* COLGRIN'S *sword stuck in a post.*

I won't say you're in my way
But I can't get to where I want to come to.

COLGRIN [*to* HOEL]. My only wife!

ANNA.   I'll take these into the sun.
Nothing ever dries in this country.

COLGRIN.   There's my weapon!
There's my dimpled sword! What do you mean, woman,
Hanging wet linen all over it? It's wrong
If it's rusty.

ANNA.   And a man is, too; and you're
So thick with rust you'd choke if you blew on yourself.

C   [17]

COLGRIN. I'm on special duty, Anna; I'm put to guard
A sad and savage Briton.

ANNA.   He needn't think
He'll be savage with me. He's caused a lot of trouble
Having to be conquered, and that's enough from him.
I shall probably get to be fond of him, but I'll never
Like him. It wouldn't be right if I did, when you think
Of all our men who've been killed killing these heathen.
And *this* isn't going to get the baby washed.

COLGRIN. What baby washed?

ANNA.   Can't I coin a phrase if I want to?
[*Exit* ANNA. *Enter* MARTINA *carrying an empty bowl.*

COLGRIN. My sword for a clothes-line!
Stand to attention. Here's my lord's daughter
Look as though you're working.

HOEL.   At what?

COLGRIN.   Here,
Plait some straw.

MARTINA.   Good morning, Colgrin.

COLGRIN.   Good-morning.
It's a bright day, lady, for the season.

MARTINA. Time, too. They made us wait for it.
I'm old with being young in a long winter.
I've almost forgotten how to walk on flowers.

COLGRIN. Everything would be all right if we'd been granted
Hibernation.

MARTINA.   We're not very favoured. The gods
Mean us to know they rule. Are your gods any
Kinder, Briton?

[18]

HOEL.   When I was a boy I was only
    Allowed to have one, though in that One, they said,
    There were three. But the altars are broken up. I've tried
    To pick away the moss to read the inscriptions
    But I've almost forgotten our language. I only know
    The god was both father and son and a brooding dove.

MARTINA. He's a Christian, Colgrin; and if you ask my mother
    She'll tell you that's worse than having no god at all.
    We have a Christian queen, though we try to keep it
    Dark, and in one of our prayers to the gods we say
    Give us our daily bread and forgive us our Queen.
    But we drove the Britons into the mountains; for years
    They've lain furtively in the setting sun,
    Those who live. Why aren't you lurking there, too?
    You should be crouching craven in a cave
    Warming your hands at the spark of your old god
    Who let you be conquered.

HOEL.   After my father was killed
    The Saxons kept me to work for them. My father
    Had always said What can one god do
    Against the many the invaders have?
    And he remembered earlier gods who still
    Harped on the hills, and hoped they would rally again.
    But they were too old. They only raised
    Infatuated echoes, and wept runnels.
    Then all the Britons were killed or fled, all
    Except my grandfather and my hip-high self.
    Him they kept for working metals which he did
    With his whole heart, forgetting the end of his race
    In a brooch design. He told me once
    How I'd been given in water to the One god.
    Soon afterwards he died, beating silver.

[19]

When I had grown the Saxons let me fight for them
And gave me a little freedom in exchange.

MARTINA. Enough for my father to take from you.
It's a pity
You had to be born a Briton. I'm forced to hate you.

HOEL. If I had been a Saxon . . .

MARTINA.   We should have killed you
To win your land, but considered you a brother.

COLGRIN. We should have killed you with consideration.
It isn't less fatal, of course, but it adds an air
Of glory, and we shake hands in Valhalla.

Enter CLODESUIDA.

CLODESUIDA. Martina, come, if you please! Two hands aren't
enough
To card and spin, and my brain goes with the wheel
Round and round in a horrible suspense.
What are you doing?

MARTINA.   Watching the herons. I'm coming.
They haunt the dregs of the mist like ghosts
Left on the yellow morning by a tide of sleep.

CLODESUIDA. Where did you take the bowl of meat?

MARTINA.   Where?

CLODESUIDA. I saw you come back from that old decaying
Tooth of a tower. And here's a string
Of bramble on your skirt, and burrs, and cleavers.
What were you doing there?

MARTINA.   I go very often.
Particularly when the house is overbearded
With splendid uncles.

CLODESUIDA.   Carrying a bowl of food?

[20]

MARTINA. Mother, I have to eat.

CLODESUIDA.   Do you have to eat
  Among bird-droppings and birds' bones and beaks
  And owl-chawn mice and dead flies? Is that
  Nicer than your uncles? The tower's a spitting-place
  For all benighted life, a filthy ruin.
  You have someone hidden there.

MARTINA.   Suppose I have . . .

CLODESUIDA. I do suppose you have; and I shall find who.
  I wear myself out securing us to the gods
  With every device that's orthodox, sacrificing
  To the hour, to the split minute of the risen sun.
  But how can I keep them kind if always
  They're being displeased by the rest of you? It isn't
  Easy to keep on the windy side of Woden
  As anyone knows. Who have you hidden in the ruin?

MARTINA. Hardly anyone at all. A very old man:
  Old enough to be his own grandfather.

CLODESUIDA. But why—

MARTINA.   I dug him up. He was rather buried.
  I found him in the quarry where it caved in.
  His beard was twisted like mist in the roots of an oak-tree,
  Beaded and bright with a slight rain, and he was crying
  Like an old wet leaf. His hands were as brown as a nest
  Of lizards, and his eyes were two pale stones
  Dropping in a dark well. I thought I couldn't
  Very well leave him where he was.

CLODESUIDA.   You should
  Have left him, until we could find out more about him.
  Is he natural? Is he good or evil? Out of the quarry!
  He might be as fatal as a toadstool.

MARTINA.   Maybe, maybe,
   Maybe. He comforts me.

CLODESUIDA.   He comforts you!
   In what way, comfortable? Now we come to it.
   What does he do?

MARTINA.   He screws up his eyes and looks
   At my hand and tells my future. It's better
   Than always having to placate the gods
   For fear something should happen. Besides, I like
   To know. He says, as far as he can remember,
   Though he has a terrible memory for names,
   His name is Merlin.

HOEL [to COLGRIN]. What did she say?

COLGRIN.   She said
   I was so thick with rust I'd choke if I blew.
   My sword for a clothes-line!

HOEL.   Merlin!

CLODESUIDA.   I only hope
   He has done no harm to us yet, whatever he is,
   Whatever his tongue clinks at, sitting with the rats.
   It's no good having gods at the door if there
   Are devils on the hearth. Your uncles, one or both,
   Shall see him.

HOEL.   She calls him Merlin. She has caught
   An echo that booms in the deepest cave of my race
   And brings it here, out into the winter light!

MARTINA. You shall see him for yourself.
   Here he comes, with the red earth still on him
   And his beard springing surprises on the breeze.
   He promised not to break his hiding. Well,
   You see how old he is. And how confused in the sun.
   With two days' growth of shadow from the tower.

Enter MERLIN.

You've broken faith. You promised you'd lie low.

[MERLIN *moves on towards* HOEL.

CLODESUIDA. What is he after?

MERLIN [*to* HOEL].   Ail i'r ar ael Eryri
Cyfartal hoewal a hi. Ar oror wir arwa.

HOEL. Peth yw . . . peth yw . . . I can't remember
How to speak. I use the words of the Saxons.

CLODESUIDA. Another heathen! Did you know he was a Briton?
Is that why you hid him from me?

MERLIN [*to* HOEL].   A British voice.
It breaks a fast of years; I roll you
Wonderfully on my tongue. I was half asleep
But I heard you. This wide harp of winter
Reverberates. I had stupidly imagined
The human landscape had left me for ever.
The face of the foam for me (I told myself)
Until I die. All your expectation
Of friendship, old man (I said to myself)
Is a wink from the eye of a bullfinch
Or the slower solemnities of a tortoise
Or a grudging goodnight from the dark lungs of a toad.
And then your voice alights on my ear. I bless you
From the bottom of my slowly budding grave.

CLODESUIDA. You must speak to my brothers before we let you
        wander
All over our land.

HOEL.   Madam, this may be Merlin.
Still Merlin. Do you understand?

MERLIN. You are surprised, I see, to find me still
Giving and taking the air. You think I should long ago

[23]

Have sunk to the golden bed of the troubled river.
But I have obstreperous garments that keep me floating.
I merely float, in a desultory, though
Delighted, kind of way. And my garments begin
To be heavy. Presently, on the surface of life,
You may observe a doting bubble, smiling
Inanely at the sun until it dissolves,
And then you'll know the time has been.

HOEL. It has gone
Already for us. We're lost and scattered.

MERLIN. Be lost
And then be found. It's an old custom of the earth
From year to year. I could do something;
But I lost my trumpet of zeal when Arthur died
And now I only wind a grey note
Of memory, and the hills are quiet.

CLODESUIDA. Did you hear
What I said to you?

MARTINA. Father has come from the house.

Enter CYMEN.

CLODESUIDA. Oh, you should be sleeping.

CYMEN. No sleep came.
An occasional shadow across my bed from a cloud
Of weariness, but the glare of the brain persisted.
Where is the Briton?

CLODESUIDA. There in the barn, there,
Talking to an old man of his tribe, or an old
Sorcerer, or some brewer of trouble.
We should rid the country of these things which aren't ourselves.

[24]

CYMEN. Rid the brain of uncertainty, rid the heart
  Of its fear.

                                        [*He goes to the barn.*

          How did this old man come here?
    The kingdom has been scoured of you islanders.
    What are you hanging about for?

MERLIN.   I pluck at my roots
    But they won't be fetched away from a world which possesses me
    Like an unforgettable woman who was once my own.
    I walk on the earth, besotted by her, waiting
    To bring to her the devotion of my dust.

HOEL.   It's Merlin. He's still among us.

CYMEN.   What is he?
    Is it one of your superstitions,
    A damned invention of the air? Tell me
    What your existence is or, by the night,
    I'll ask your flesh with a sharper edge to the question.
    Come on, now; are you superannuated god
    Or working devil, or mere entangled man?

MERLIN. No god, I hope; that would take too much
    Endurance. Whatever man may be
    I am that thing, though my birth, I've been given to believe,
    Had some darkness in it. But then, which of us
    Can say he is altogether free of a strain
    Of hell in his blood? My father could be called
    Pure man, if such a thing existed.

CYMEN.   Then
    What powers pursue us here? You know this island
    Thoroughly. Parade your spirits, good
    And bad, and I'll identify the mischief!

[25]

CLODESUIDA. Will you ask *them*, men of the race
We conquered?

MARTINA.   Ask the prisoner
If he isn't a Christian. He's a godless Christian
Even if he can't remember.

CLODESUIDA.   Why can't we get rid of them
Once and for all? The gods will strike at them
And everyone knows how carelessly they aim. The blow
May fall on us.

COLGRIN.   Colgrin will catch it, Colgrin
Is sure to catch it. The rest of the world will dodge
And I shall be in the way.

CYMEN.   I'll ask the louse
In the filthy shirt of a corpse in the bottom of a ditch
If I can learn what it is I've learnt to dread.
I lay on my bed and felt it stand with its feet
Planted on either side of my heart, and I looked
Up the tower of its body to find the face
To know if it meant to help or hinder,
But it was blotted out by a shield of thunder.
Am I to sacrifice without end and then
Be given no peace? The skirts of the gods
Drag in our mud. We feel the touch
And take it to be a kiss. But they see we soil them
And twitch themselves away. Name to me
What mocked me with a mood of mercy and therefore
Defeat. Who desired that?

MERLIN.   Who, apart
From ourselves, can see any difference between
Our victories and our defeats, dear sir?
Not beast, nor bird, nor even the anticipating
Vulture watching for the battle's end,

[26]

Nor a single mile of devoted dispassionate ground.
All indifferent. Much more so your gods
Who live without the world, who never feel
As the world feels in springtime the stab of the spear
And the spurt of golden blood,
Winter's wound-in-the-side, the place where life begins.
Nothing, it seems, cares for your defeat.

CLODESUIDA. How did I say these Britons would answer you?
It shames us to stand and listen. Didn't we conquer them?

MERLIN. Quest and conquest and quest again. It might well
Make you fretful if you weren't expecting it.

CYMEN. You are conquered. Both you or this boy
I can destroy now, and no questions asked.

MERLIN. Death is what conquers the killer, not the killed.
How pleasant it is to talk, even
In your language. I have a way—your daughter
May have told you—of looking ahead, having made
My peace with Time, at some expense to my soul.
It's curious to know that in the course
Of the movement of years which wears away distinction,
You, and moreover your conquerors, will bear
Kindly and as though by nature our name, the British
Name, and all the paraphernalia, legend
And history, as though you were our widow
Not our conqueror. And well may the weeds become you.

CYMEN. You're a hideous old wiseacre
Of sheepbitten kale. But give me an answer.
If, as you imagine, our gods have no care
Whether we win or lose, what cuckoo power
Is it that usurps the nest of my soul?

MERLIN. You ask an old pagan? Old Merlin, old
Eternal suckling, who cannot drag his lips

Away from the breast of the earth, even to grow
Into the maturity of heaven. Nothing can wean him
Until his mother puts upon her nipple
The vinegar of death, though, when I walked
Between the dog-rose hedges of my manhood,
It was in a Christian land: in Arthur's land.
There I gleamed in the iris of creation's
Eye, and there I laughed as a man should,
Between the pillars of my ribs in the wide
Nave of my chest. A Christian land. There
It was, and old Joseph's faithful staff
Breaking into scarlet bud in the falling snow.
But, as I said at the time, the miracle
Was commonplace: staves of chestnut wood
And maywood and the like perform it every year.
And men broke their swords in the love of battle,
And broke their hearts in the love of women,
And broke the holy bread in the love of God.
I saw them ride away between their loves
Into a circle of the snow-white wind
And so into my head's old yellow world
Of bone.

CYMEN.   Your Christian land was weak, it shook
Down, it burnt, its ash was blown
Into our food and drink. What I'm inflicted with
Is strong, destroying me with a cry of love,
A violence of humility arrogantly
Demanding all I am or possess or have ambitions for,
Insistent as a tocsin which was sounded
When the sun first caught on fire, and ever since
Clangs alarm with a steady beat in the wild
Night of history. This doesn't come

From the watery light of what you think you remember.
A lashing logic drags me away from my gods.
Let it face me like a man!

MERLIN.   It may be already
This power has faced you like a man, on a certain
Century's peak from which the circling low land
Is, to eternity, surveyed. Still, still,
Earth winds delicious arms; it isn't strange
Our human eyes should close upon her, like a flower
Closing on a globe of dew, and wish to see
Nothing but this. And here am I
Doting into oblivion.

CLODESUIDA.   Send him off,
With his ancient ramifications; go to sleep
And be well.

CYMEN [to HOEL]. Do I have to come to you again?
You, a speck of the dust which three of our generations
Have marched over: what light flung from you
To me? Why did my strength startle from your
Futility?

HOEL.   On my soul, I've done nothing against you
Except to make war. I've known nothing except
Your mercy; that indeed was a kind of light to me.
I want to live, having a life in me
Which seems to demand it.

MERLIN.   Having a death in him, too:
That death by drowning in the river of his baptism
From which he rose a dripping Christian child
In a land which had become a grave to us all,
Though in that grave of Britain old Merlin, for one,
Was happy enough because he could hold, both hill

[29]

And valley, his leafy love in his arms,
Old pagan that he is.

HOEL.   The weather of twenty
Years has blown me dry, and long lost me
All the charms I ever had of that.

MERLIN. The spirit is very tenacious of such water.

CYMEN. The spirit again! You nod and look beyond me,
And pretend to know nothing. Do you dare to say
The world has a secret direction passing the gods?
And does it run through me? [*To* CLODESUIDA.] Take me from
   them.
I'm mad, mad to talk to the slaves.

CLODESUIDA.   Rest, Cymen.

CYMEN. I am alive and so there is no rest.

CLODESUIDA. It's you who churn up the air; the air itself
Is as unruffled as ever. Trust our gods
And put these heathen to work.

                    Enter ANNA.

ANNA.   Master, master, master!
Where is the master? The wolves, the savages!
An old woman's no use! Oh, the master!

CYMEN. What's the matter?

ANNA.   So many wolves, the fields
Are a bear-garden—ma'am, your brothers!—grey,
Snarling, vicious, a terrible pack—they're into
The sheep!

CYMEN.   The sheep!

CLODESUIDA.   Brothers, help, help us,
Wake, the wolves have come!

[30]

ANNA.   The sheep and the lambs,
   All we have!

MARTINA.   In the daylight, in daylight, too!
   What could have brought them?

ANNA.   Why, hunger, hunger, the appetite,
   The spite of the belly!

          Enter TADFRID, OSMER, QUICHELM, *and* CHELDRIC.

OSMER.   What's the cry?

CLODESUIDA.   The wolves!
   They're falling on the flock!

TADFRID.   So it begins,
   Bad-luck already.

OSMER.   Down to them, then, and save
   What's still for saving.
               [CYMEN *has already snatched* COLGRIN'S *sword and gone;*
               HOEL *also, ahead of him. Now the rest follow, shouting to
               scatter the wolves.*

ANNA.   I'm fit for nothing now
   But whisking eggs, I'm trembling so.
   Why should such things be? Such fangs, I have
   Sharp pains in the back just to have seen them
   Gnashing in the light. [*Seeing* COLGRIN]: Why are you here,
   You, taking up space as though time didn't begin
   Until the day after to-morrow? Do all legs move
   Except the two that keep the ground away from you?
   Why don't you go and help?

COLGRIN.   My dear, good woman,
   I'm here on duty.

ANNA.   What duty would you mean,
   I wonder? The prisoner's gone.

                         [31]

COLGRIN. All the more reason
Why the other half of the arrangement should stand.
If the horse gets out of the stable it doesn't mean
The stable is justified in following.
I'm a man who can be relied on.

ANNA. So you are.
Well, at least when your time comes to be buried
They'll have no trouble keeping you under the ground.
But why should wolves be set upon us? Men
Make enough misfortunes for themselves, without
Natural calamities happening as well.
The old gentleman agrees.

MERLIN. Considerable
Age makes me nod; I neither agree
Nor disagree. I'm too near-sighted now
To be able to distinguish one thing from another,
The storm-swollen river from the tear-swollen eyes,
Or the bare cracked earth from the burnt-out face,
Or the forest soughing from the sighing heart.
What is in one is in the other, a mood
Of rage which turns upon itself to savage
Its own body, since there's nothing except itself
On which anger can alight; it sinks into time
Like a sword into snow
And the roots receive all weathers and subsist,
And the seasons are reconciled. When, years ago,
The Romans fell away from our branching roads
Like brazen leaves, answering
The hopeless windy trumpets from their home,
Your tribes waged winter upon us, till our limbs
Ached with the carving cold. You blackened
The veins of the valleys with our dried blood. And at last

[32]

Your lives croaked like crows on a dead bough
And the echoes clanged against you. But I can hear
Faintly on the twittering sea a sail
Moving greatly where the waves, like harvest-home,
Come hugely on our coast: the men of Rome
Returning, bringing God, winter over, a breath
Of green exhaled from the hedges, the wall of sky
Breached by larksong. Primrose and violet
And all frail privileges of the early ground
Gather like pilgrims in the aisles of the sun.
A ship in full foliage rides in
Over the February foam, and rests
Upon Britain.

COLGRIN.   He's in the clouds, you see; he's away
On his own; he's blowing about like the hairs in his beard.

ANNA. Maybe, yes, and maybe also his beard
Has caught on something. He seems to have brought
The other side of the hill into his head.
It's good to see—we anticipate little enough—
And certainly to-day, I noticed myself,
Winter is wearing thin; it's beginning to show
The flowering body through.

COLGRIN.   It's a hard time,
The spring; it makes me lose all my energy.

Enter CLODESUIDA.

CLODESUIDA. Did you see it, did ever your eyes? He must be as
     wild
As an animal in his heart! Who ever saw
Such wrestling between hand and claw?

ANNA.   Such what,
Such wrestling? I hadn't hard enough eyes

D   [33]

To put them again on those poor bleating lambs.
Are the wolves away now? Are the wolves away?
I still shake for the sake of those sheep.

CLODESUIDA.   The wolves
Are beaten off. But the Briton killed the grimmest,
The greatest: with his hands, with his hands as bare
As mine: met and mauled the scavenger, with a grip
Under the blood and froth of the jaws, he shook
And choked the howling out of its fangs
And forced it to a carcase. It was horror
And hope and terror and triumph to see it.

ANNA. The boy? The Briton? with bare hands?

MERLIN.   Like a shepherd
With a lion.

COLGRIN.   With his bare hands?

ANNA.   It's just as well
To hang the wet linen on your sword,
You heavy hero on my conscience.

        Enter TADFRID, OSMER, QUICHELM, *and* CHELDRIC.

CLODESUIDA.   It's a tale
I'll tell to my grave! My heart is hammering
And still hugging the fearful sport of the struggle.
What shall we do to reward him?

OSMER.   Reward him? his death
Can reward him. Who's the fool who's going to kiss
Future trouble? Who does, deserves to lie
With the grass growing up through a crack in the skull.

CLODESUIDA. What do you mean? Didn't he enlist himself
Against our disaster?

TADFRID.   But in what power's name?
Osmer fears—

[34]

OSMER.   And very properly fears.
I'm not quite a child in this cleft-stick of life.

Enter CYMEN.

CYMEN. Are you still rolling your marbles of thunder?
I hear what you say. Still breaking wind to make
A hurricane. I am very tired.

OSMER.   And so
Are we all with anxiety. And so no doubt
Are the crouching gods who contain their final leap
Waiting for wisdom from us.

TADFRID.   And not holding
For long, now that the first roar has come.

CYMEN. That may be. I know well enough
The weight of the silence that's on our shoulders now.
I move under it like the moving mole
That raises the hackles of dead leaves.
Under me, silence; round me, silence, air,
The wind hushing the world to hear
The wind hushing the world; and over me,
Silence upon silence upon silence,
Unuttering vapour, unutterable void.
What do you want me to do?

OSMER.   Make retribution
Before we're godsmitten again.

TADFRID.   A sacrifice.

OSMER. The only possible sacrifice, the Briton.

CLODESUIDA. Can they be right, Cymen? Certainly
We must do what is necessary, though when
I saw the wolf destroyed—

OSMER.   As now you shall see
Our luck's neck fractured, unless we act.

[35]

The Briton sprang on the back of a punishment
Justly put upon us by the gods.

TADFRID. That's so. And by what muscle, except a devil's,
Could he elbow himself between our gods and us?

OSMER. It's perfectly proper that we should contest our punish-
ment,
If we can. The gods relish a knock or two
Before they lean back and insist on being
Propitiated. But by no right does this Briton
Break in and ruffle them beyond all hope.
His demon rams him to it to make our world
The worse for us.

QUICHELM.   We've got to be free of him.
Cut him to quiet. He's a flint that's going to skag us.
Hit the spark of life out of him, father.

TADFRID. What else but a power of the dark would send him
Scudding into the teeth and talons
Of a probable death, for us, his enemies?
If you let him live among us—

          [*Enter* HOEL, *helped by* MARTINA. *His shoulders have been
          clawed by the wolf. They walk across to the barn, watched in
          silence by the others.*

CYMEN.   I will sacrifice.

OSMER. Then back we come to easy breathing
And a chance of pleasure.

CLODESUIDA.   Let me think of the harm
He would do us, his brain's blackened teeth,
And not sicken at his killing. What the gods
Want we'll give them, even though our blood
Freezes.

[36]

CYMEN. I will sacrifice.
  I'll pay off whatever dark debts there are
  And come to the morning, square. I am tired, tired
  Of being ground between the staring stones
  Of air and earth. I'll satisfy the silence.
  Bring me one of the white goats.

TADFRID *and* OSMER.   A goat?

CYMEN. One silence of death is as deep as another
  To satisfy the silence. It will do
  To patch wherever a whisper from above
  Can still creep out. Bring me the goat.

CLODESUIDA.   But this
  Can't please them if they demand the Briton?

OSMER. It's livestock thrown away.

TADFRID.   Look, he goes
  To pray to them.

CYMEN [*at the altar*]. Gods, our gods, gods
  Of the long forced-march of our blood's generations
  Dead and living. Goaders, grappling gods,
  Whose iron feet pace on thunder's floor
  Up and down in the hall where chaos groaned
  And bore creation sobbing. Boding gods,
  Who broad in the universe consume our days
  Like food, and crunch us, good and bad,
  Like bones. What do I do by sacrifice?
  The blood flows, the ground soaks it up,
  The poisoned nightshade grows, the fears go on,
  The dread of doom gropes into the bowels,
  And hope, with her ambitious shovel, sweats
  To dig the pit which swallows us at last.
  The sacrifice is despair and desperation!

[37]

The deed of death is done and done and always
To do, death and death and death; and still
We cannot come and stand between your knees.
Why? By what stroke was the human flesh
Hacked so separate from the body of life
Beyond us? You make us to be the eternal alien
In our own world. Then I submit. Separation
To separation! Dedicated stones
Can lie asunder until the break is joined!

       [CYMEN *throws down the stones of the altar. The rest, except*
       HOEL, *throw themselves in horror on to the ground.*

Answer, then, answer! I am alone, without hope.
The outlaw, no longer the groveller on the knee.
Silence me! Come down and silence me!
Then at least I shall have some kind of part
With all the rest.

                [*They wait.*]
             Not even that?
Is separation between man and gods
So complete? Can't you even bring me to silence?

       [*A voice from a short way off is heard calling 'Cymen!*
       Cymen of the Copse!' CYMEN stands startled. The rest raise
       themselves partly from the ground in apprehension. The voice
       calls, again, nearer.

CYMEN. What is it? Who is it? I am here on my ground.

           Enter a MESSENGER.

MESSENGER. Cymen of the Copse, is he here?

CYMEN.   I'm that man.

MESSENGER. You're summoned to the general assemblage
  Of all householders, copyholders, smallholders, and tenant-
    farmers,
  At the command of Ethelbert, lord and king of Kent,

To receive the person and words of Augustine
Exponent of the Christian god.
Proper precautions are being taken, and all
Provision made, to protect each person present
From being taken at a disadvantage
By the craft of any spirit whatsoever,
Evil or good. Therefore you will take your stand
Not under the king's roof
But where the air keeps open house
And the sun in the sky suffers all for all,
Or at least if any charms are set afoot
They will be less concentrated, owing to the wind.

CYMEN. Am I called to the king?

MESSENGER.   You assemble on the western hill
To receive the person and words—

MERLIN.   Of Augustine
Sent by Gregory of Rome who on a market-day
Saw angels where we see our enemies.

ANNA. He knew, that's what he said, he saw them coming
In a ship full of primroses from Rome!

CYMEN [*to the* MESSENGER]. I am slow to understand you. I was
    up
On the bare back of dreadful thoughts. Who chose
That you should come to me now? What ground
Am I dismounting onto, your ordinary summons
To the king?

MESSENGER. You find it unpleasant? The news, I see,
Has reached you already, and distaste, I suppose,
Is understandable, though all you're supposed to do
Is to sit and give the appearance of paying attention
Out of consideration for the queen.

[39]

CLODESUIDA. She would like to make heathen of us all!
    We're on poor enough terms with the gods as it is
    Without seeming to keep open minds.

OSMER.   They're only
    Hesitating over the choice of weapons
    They mean to use against us.

TADFRID.   The sky is clear,
    The sun still shines, but there's little doubt
    Their indignation is mounting under the self-control
    Of the horizon. Let the king indulge the queen
    If it keeps her wife-minded, but here more than ever
    We've got to remain rigid with reality.

MESSENGER. In my opinion you're taking devoutness too hard.
    The gods won't object to our being a bit diplomatic.
    I'll leave you to make your way, Cymen of the Copse.

CYMEN. Time makes my way, and I go on with time.
    What is contrives what will be. Yes, I shall come.

                                    [Exit the MESSENGER.

TADFRID. Will you go and leave us now to suffer
    In whatever suffering comes of your blasphemy?

OSMER. Let him go.

CLODESUIDA.   But now of all times isn't the time;
    He's so wretched from his brainstorm of wrong,
    Every pore of his skin's wide open to punishment.

OSMER. Let him go, let him go.

CYMEN [to HOEL].   Your god has come, perhaps,
    Or lies in wait on the lips of a man from Rome.
    Strange. As though a spirit in you, like
    A wild fowl hiding in the mere of your flesh,
    Heard the sound far off and flew up clamouring
    Rousing a spirit in me. We're in the path

[40]

Of change. And I must go to meet the change,
Being unable to live unaltered.

HOEL.   Is it true,
Indeed? Is the One god making his way again
In through the many?

CYMEN.   I go to know.
I go to dare my arm into the thicket
To know what lifts its head there, whether rose
Or tiger, or tiger and rose together.
Be undisturbed, my dear disturbed wife.
If I rock, it's with the rocking of the world;
It will get me to sleep in time. As for the rest of you,
Wait, with a certain degree of trust.
Yes, you can build up the altar again if you must.
It will be somewhere to sit when the days are warmer.
Meanwhile, the silence keep you, the silence
Be gracious unto you and give you peace.

> [*Exit* CYMEN. TADFRID *and* OSMER *have started, and now
> continue, to rebuild the altar.* CLODESUIDA *watches* CYMEN
> *on his way.*

CLODESUIDA. Should he go? He walks steadily enough now,
Very much as he does behind a plough. Is this only
A lull on his brain? Can he avoid trouble
After what he has done?

TADFRID.   The air is clearer without him.
And let's hope the bloodshot eyes above us
Have followed him and don't still fix on us here.

QUICHELM. It was awful to watch him. We must make it right with
    the gods.
They can't expect sons to carry the blame for fathers.
Would they make us suffer because of our blood?

[41]

HOEL. Yes;
Or from whose example would men have learnt that trick?

OSMER. You'll scream yourself sorry if we turn ourselves to you.

MARTINA [to HOEL]. You're still a Briton, even though I have
Washed your wounds. Lie low, and don't make trouble.

CHELDRIC. Our mother's blood flows in us too, uncle,
And mother fears the gods. Won't that be taken
Into account?

CLODESUIDA. The same with the gods as with men;
Women are only camp-followers, they take
Our obedience for granted. If *we* blasphemed
They would pinch our cheeks and resume the course of history
As though nothing had happened. We succeed or suffer
According to our men.

ANNA. Then I roughen my hands
For a fine lark.

CLODESUIDA. Day's work is still to do,
Whatever the day's doom. I have no hope
To be able to know what hope to have. My hands
Can only draw their everyday conclusions.

ANNA. Yes, we must busy ourselves, and try to forget
The complication of what's up there beyond us.
[*To* COLGRIN.] Are you still rooted to the spot with duty?

COLGRIN. Unavoidably static.

OSMER. Get onto your work.

COLGRIN. But suppose the prisoner—

OSMER. Suppose
You do what you're told and quick.

COLGRIN. Quick? I'll suppose
Anything once; but that's not how I am.
I was born midway between the quick and the dead.

[42]

ANNA. Budge over a little farther from the grave.

[*Exeunt* CLODESUIDA, COLGRIN, *and* ANNA.

TADFRID. What do we mean to do? The altar stones
Now stand as they were. But not to them.
To them the stones are still pitching and blundering
From jutting god to jutting god, down
The scowling scarp of their everlasting memory.
They say the gods were formed
Out of the old hurt pride of rejected chaos
Which is still lusting for the body of the world we walk on.

OSMER. If they'll give us time and the merest shove
In the lucky direction we're leaning to already,
We shall be able to elude the allegiance to Cymen
Which is such an obstacle in the way of well-doing,
Nullify guilt and mollify the gods
And bury the brat's guts for good in the ground.
You shall see; it will be as I say
If the gods give us time.

TADFRID.   But Cymen claimed
His death to himself.

OSMER.   We'll do it in his name;
If a moment which insists on action
Comes while he's away, he would expect us
To live the moment for him.

TADFRID.   If the crisis came.

QUICHELM. What's the talk? Do you think we're in for the worst?
Do you see any hope that we can relax
Now that father's gone, or what's your guess?

CHELDRIC. Isn't the danger less?

OSMER.   Come away from here.
I've got a screw of courage you can chew;

[43]

We're not committed to damnation yet.
Let your sister stay. We'll pray, with a certain purpose.
          [*Exeunt* TADFRID, OSMER, QUICHELM, *and* CHELDRIC.

MARTINA. They hate you; and that's easy to understand.
  We have existence on such hard terms,
  As though birth into the world had been a favour
  Instantly regretted. We haven't the air
  To spare for strangers. I hope the claw-marks heal.
  I've done my best for them.

HOEL.   Thanks. Are you going in?

MARTINA. Of course. There's nothing to keep me here.

HOEL. No; there's nothing.

MARTINA.   What do you want?

HOEL.   I wonder
  What it was that came and wielded your father and left me
  Alive?

MARTINA. I'll not worry about my father,
  Nor my mother, nor my uncles nor, between ourselves,
  The gods. The universe is too ill-fitting
  And large. I am very careful about small
  Things, such as wearing green in the third month
  Or bringing blackthorn under the roof;
  But the big things, such as gods, must look after themselves.

HOEL. Still, I'm curious about the One god.
  I've never completely shaken him off. He seems
  To insist.

MARTINA. You're a born heathen. Get some sleep.
  You look too tired to be hated
  And that won't do at all.

HOEL.   Do you have to hate me?

MARTINA. It isn't one of my easiest duties. But how else
   Can we keep our footing or our self-esteem?
   Now sleep and look malignant when you wake.

HOEL. Sleep, yes. My fields need rain. Sleep
   Can drench down and welcome.

                   [Exit MARTINA. HOEL *lies in the straw and sleeps.*

MERLIN.   Welcome, sleep;
   Welcome into the winter head of the world
   The sleep of Spring, which grows dreams,
   Nodding trumpets, blowing bells,
   A jingle of birds whenever the sun moves,
   Never so lightly; all dreams,
   All dreams out of slumbering rock:
   Lambs in a skittle prance, the hobbling rook
   Like a witch picking sticks,
   And pinnacle-ears the hare
   Ladling himself along in the emerald wheat:
   All dreams out of the slumbering rock,
   Each dream answering to a shape
   Which was in dream before the shapes were shapen;
   Each growing obediently to a form,
   To its own sound, shrill or deep, to a life
   In water or air, in light or night or mould;
   By sense or thread perceiving,
   Eye, tendril, nostril, ear; to the shape of the dream
   In the ancient slumbering rock.
   And above the shapes of life, the shape
   Of death, the singular shape of the dream dissolving,
   Into which all obediently come.
   And above the shape of death, the shape of the will
   Of the slumbering rock, the end of the throes of sleep
   Where the stream of the dream wakes in the open eyes

[45]

Of the sea of the love of the morning of the God.
Here's an old man whiling away a spring
Day, with thoughts so far beyond the moss
He roots in, they're as nebulous
As the muted flute of a dove to the root of a tree.
Never mind. However warmly I curl
My tail around my feet and admire myself
Reflected in the nut before I bite,
Still I observe the very obdurate pressure
Edging men towards a shape beyond
The shape they know. Now and then, by a spurt
Of light, they manage the clumsy approximation,
Overturn it, turn again, refashion
Nearer the advising of their need.
Always the shape lying over the life.
Pattern of worm in the sand was not the shape,
Nor the booming body of enormous beast,
Nor the spread fan of the blue-eyed quivering tail,
Nor the weave of the nest, nor the spun wheel of the web,
Nor the maze and cellarage of honey, nor
The charts and maps of men. The shape shone
Like a faint circle round a moon
Of hazy gods, and age by age
The gods reformed according to the shape,
According to the shape that was a word,
According to Thy Word. Here's more than half
A pagan whiling away the spring sunshine.
The morning has come within a distant sight
Of evening, and the wandering shadows begin
To stretch their limbs a little. I shall move
Myself, into the quiet of the tumbling tower,
For an hour or two of casual obliteration
And break more ground for dreams.

[*Exit* MERLIN. *Enter, after a pause,* MARTINA *with a bowl of food. She goes to* HOEL, *who is still asleep.*

MARTINA. You're even less of an enemy when you sleep.
Wake up. You've gone where we're all of one size.
Bring yourself back and know your station.

HOEL.   Yes?
This isn't where I sleep. Why is my heart
So heavy?

MARTINA. Here is food. You have to be
A good enemy and eat.

HOEL.   You went indoors.
I thought you might not come back again.

MARTINA. Aren't you hungry?

HOEL.   Perhaps. From where I sit
On the kerb of sleep I feel I know you better
Than I did before. Take the bowl in your hands
And let me eat the food from there.

MARTINA. Am I your servant?

HOEL.   I'm your servant. I slept
When you said sleep, and I'll eat like a tame swan
Out of your hands.

MARTINA.   Too black for a swan,
You'd make me a good shadow. I'll ask my father
To give you to be my personal shadow,
To walk behind me in the morning, and before me
In the evening, and at noon I'll have you
Under my feet.

HOEL.   I shall adjust myself
Easily to noon.

MARTINA.   You'll feel humiliated
And bite the dust.

[47]

HOEL.   I shall feel delighted
  And kiss the sole of your foot.

MARTINA.   It's clear you're nothing
  But a poor-spirited Briton if you're willing
  To become a girl's shadow.

HOEL.   Yes, indeed;
  A poor-spirited Briton; you remind me
  In good time.

MARTINA.   But a Briton who, if he were a Jute,
  Would be brave and agreeable. So be glad of that.

HOEL. What simple-witted things the affections are,
  That can't perceive whether people are enemies
  Or friends. You would think the strong distinction
  Between race and race would be clear even to the heart
  Though it does lie so retired
  Beating its time away in the human breast.

MARTINA. You talk of nothing that interests me. Eat
  Your food.

        Enter TADFRID, OSMER, QUICHELM, *and* CHELDRIC.

OSMER.   You see, she has gone to him again.
  It's the way I said it would be. His damned contagion
  Spreads.

TADFRID. It flies first to the weakest place.
  That girl sees nothing but an eye and a mouth
  And doesn't care.

QUICHELM.   She can go and eat grass
  Before I call her sister again.

OSMER.   She gives us
  The grounds for getting him where the gods want him.
  He is ours and his blood's as good as gone to them.

[48]

If we hesitated now even Cymen would say
We were as puny as pulp.

MARTINA [*to* HOEL]. You look so sad.

[*She kisses him on the forehead.*

QUICHELM [*leaping forward*]. Leper-flesh!

CHELDRIC. He snared her!

MARTINA. What's so wrong?

QUICHELM. You and the flicker of your rutting eyes are wrong!

OSMER. Toleration has gone to the limit. Now
We strike. You black pawn of the devil's game,
Come out.

HOEL. Why, what is it you mean to do?

OSMER. Make much of you, make a god's meal of you,
And make our peace with you, with you as peacemaker,
And not too soon. It's a quiet future for you.
I said come out.

MARTINA. No! My father said he was not to be harmed!

OSMER. He wouldn't say it now. Uncertainty
Has dandled us enough to make us sick
For life. Now we're not going to fob
The gods off any longer.

QUICHELM. Must we wait?
Give me the word, and I'll fetch his cringing carcase
Out for you.

MARTINA. Don't dare to touch him!

TADFRID. Niece,
We must submit to the wish of what we worship.
We rid the world of an evil. Let's not rage.
We do what's demanded of us, with solemnity,
Without passion. Fetch him out.

E [49]

MARTINA.   No, you shall not!

OSMER. Take her!

[CHELDRIC *drags back* MARTINA *and holds her.* OSMER *and* QUICHELM *fetch* HOEL *to the centre of the stage.*

MARTINA.   Cowards!

HOEL.   Let me live, do, do
Let me live.

TADFRID. Bring him to the tree; we'll offer him
In Woden's way, the Woden death. Come on;
We'll be well out of our fear.

MARTINA.   Cowards, cowards,
Cowards, sneakthieves, only dare with father gone!

[*They fasten him to the tree with his arms spread.*

HOEL. Is this the end indeed? Where now for me?

MARTINA. Father! Father!

HOEL.   Son and the brooding dove.
Call him again.

MARTINA.   Father!

OSMER.   We set this house
Free from fear and guilt and the working of darkness.

QUICHELM. We clean our hearts.

TADFRID.   The sun flows on the spear.
The spear answers the sun. They are one, and go
To the act in the concord of a sacrifice.

HOEL. Death, be to me like a hand that shades
My eyes, helping me to see
Into the light.

[50]

OSMER. Woden, we pay your dues
  Of blood.

TADFRID. Receive it and receive us back
  Into a comfortable security.
            [OSMER *makes to plunge the spear.* MARTINA *breaks free of*
            CHELDRIC *and crying 'No!' tries to prevent the stroke.*
            [*Enter* CLODESUIDA.

CLODESUIDA. Have they struck at us again, the gods?
  What more
  Have we to bear?

MARTINA.   Look, look!

CLODESUIDA [*covering her eyes*]. It has to be
  For our good; we must endure these things, to destroy
  Error, and so the gods will warm towards us.

QUICHELM. Here comes my father home!

OSMER.   Well, home he comes.
  We're in the right.

TADFRID.   He will understand this tree
  By reason of our plight had to bear such fruit.
            [*Enter* CYMEN. *He goes towards the barn, near which*
            CLODESUIDA *is now standing.*

CYMEN. Clodesuida, a peaceful heart to you now.
  I am well; I have seen our terrible gods come down
  To beg the crumbs which fall from our sins, their only
  Means of life. This evening you and I
  Can walk under the trees and be ourselves
  Together, knowing that this wild day has gone
  For good. Where is the Briton? You still think
  You must be afraid and see in him
  The seed of a storm. But I have heard

[51]

Word of his God, and felt our lonely flesh
Welcome to creation. The fearful silence
Became the silence of great sympathy,
The quiet of God and man in the mutual word.
And never again need we sacrifice, on and on
And on, greedy of the gods' goodwill
But always uncertain; for sacrifice
Can only perfectly be made by God
And sacrifice has so been made, by God
To God in the body of God with man,
On a tree set up at the four crossing roads
Of earth, heaven, time, and eternity
Which meet upon that cross. I have heard this;
And while we listened, with our eyes half-shut
Facing the late sun, above the shoulder
Of the speaking man I saw the cross-road tree,
The love of the God hung on the motes and beams
Of light, as though—

MARTINA.   Father!

[CYMEN *turns and sees* HOEL.

CYMEN.   Is it also here?
Can the sun have written it so hotly on to my eyes—
What have you done?

OSMER.   The unavoidable moment
Came while you were gone—

CYMEN.   What have you done?

TADFRID. Would *you* not break the body of our evil?

CYMEN. I will tell you what I know. Cut him down.
O pain of the world!—I will tell you what I know.
Bring him here to me.

CLODESUIDA.   We have to live.

[52]

CYMEN. We have still to learn to live.

[They bring HOEL *to* CYMEN.
They say
The sacrifice of God was brought about
By the blind anger of men, and yet God made
Their blindness their own saving and lonely flesh
Welcome to creation. Briton, boy,
Your God is here, waiting in this land again.
Forgive me for the sorrow of this world.

MARTINA. You haven't made the sorrow—

CYMEN.   All make all:
For while I leave one muscle of my strength
Undisturbed, or hug one coin of ease
Or private peace while the huge debt of pain
Mounts over all the earth,
Or, fearing for myself, take half a stride
Where I could leap; while any hour remains
Indifferent, I have no right or reason
To raise a cry against this blundering cruelty
Of man.

OSMER. Shall we let the light of our lives
Be choked by darkness?

CYMEN.   Osmer,
What shall we do? We are afraid
To live by rule of God, which is forgiveness,
Mercy, and compassion, fearing that by these
We shall be ended. And yet if we could bear
These three through dread and terror and terror's doubt,
Daring to return good for evil without thought
Of what will come, I cannot think
We should be the losers. Do we believe
There is no strength in good or power in God?

[53]

God give us courage to exist in God,
And lonely flesh be welcome to creation.
Carry him in.

> [*As they carry* HOEL *away*, CYMEN, CLODESUIDA, *and*
> MARTINA *following, the voices of Augustine's men are heard*
> *singing.*

THE END

PRINTED IN
GREAT BRITAIN
AT THE
UNIVERSITY PRESS
OXFORD
BY
CHARLES BATEY
PRINTER
TO THE
UNIVERSITY